# REAL
# MERCY

*Mary, Forgiveness, and Trust*

Published by Scepter Publishers, Inc.
info@scepterpublishers.org
www.scepterpublishers.org
800-322-8773
New York

All rights reserved.

Translated by Maria Masterson
Text and cover design by Rose Design

Printed in the United States of America

ISBN: 978-1-59417-247-2

# REAL MERCY

## Mary, Forgiveness, and Trust

### JACQUES PHILIPPE

 Scepter

# Contents

·༺༻·

# INTRODUCTION

·✍·

P ope Benedict has aptly reminded us, "We must trust in the mighty power of God's mercy. We are all sinners, but his grace transforms us and makes us new." Our call to transformation by the power of God's love and mercy has been made newly apparent to us in the last century. Through the diary of St. Faustina Kowalska, the installation of Divine Mercy Sunday by our beloved St. Pope John Paul II, and again through the Jubilee of Mercy announced by Pope Francis, there is a thematic continuance that is as modern as it is spiritually essential: to pull away from sin, grab hold of the loving mercy of the Lord, and rest in the peace that only he can give. Even the recent reemergence of the devotion to Our Lady Undoer of Knots, made popular by Pope Francis, reminds us that, through the help of Our Lady, the Lord's mercy is always at work: forgiving trespasses, healing wounds, repairing hearts, and undoing life's snags that are inevitable through our human frailty.

In fact, Fr. Philippe delves deeply into the role of Mary as a conduit for God's mercy. He tells us that her role is "discreet" yet vital, as the Mediatrix of All Graces and the one who understands God best. Her role, ever in the background, is to impress a mother's compassion upon her children, and nothing makes her happier than to see God's mercy bestowed and accepted.

And this is the key: Because of our freedom we must not only recognize God's mercy but accept it. Fr. Philippe focuses on acceptance (or trust), because we so often lack humility, self-forgiveness, and self-abandonment to his love, the portals to the flow of God's endless mercy.

As we work on becoming People of Mercy, accepting God's flowing graces and bestowing our own mercy on others, the sacrament of reconciliation continues to play a pivotal role in this exchange of love between God and man. As

Fr. Philippe says, "Every time that Jesus looks at us, he sets us free, he gives us a new life. Let us allow Jesus to look at us." Confession is an intimate conversation between the loving God and his child, during which he sets his gaze on our bowed heads seeking humility and forgiveness. The more we accept his healing gaze, the more we can come to know and love him. What a precious gift, not to be forgotten or tucked into the corners of our daily existence!

This book is a gift. We are invited by the Lord to explore the depths of his mercy through the wisdom and keen spiritual sense of Fr. Philippe. Let us all accept Jesus's look of merciful tenderness as he "opens us up to a path of life."

# Chapter One

# MERCY AND THE MOTHER OF GOD

*A homily given on December 8, 2015, at Thomas More College, Merrimack, New Hampshire*

Today, on December 8, we are entering into the Year of Mercy. Pope Francis wanted this year to begin on the feast of the Immaculate Conception of the Virgin Mary. On this day we celebrate her beauty, her purity, and her freedom from every form of sin, a sign of God's victory.

Pope Francis included this sentence in his Bull: "The mystery of the Immaculate Conception shows that the mercy of God will always be greater than the sin of men." This is a statement of hope. The mercy of God will always be greater than our sins, and this is what we contemplate in the mystery of the Virgin Mary.

For this reason, the Virgin Mary can help us to receive all of the graces of this year. This is what I'm going to try to share with you in a simple way. Many doors in churches and cathedrals will open in the coming days throughout the world. Millions of people will cross these thresholds, and this will be a great grace. There will be many healings and conversions, many graces of repentance, peace, and consolation.

## GOD'S MERCY

We need to give thanks to God for this year. Mary herself is the door of mercy because through her the mercy of God entered into the world. We can say that Jesus is the mercy of the Father in person, because through the person of Jesus, the merciful love of the Father was revealed in order to reach everyone—in their sin, their wounds, and their weakness.

The mercy of God is completely free. It is an abundant source of tenderness, generosity, and unconditional love. We have no need to buy it, no need to merit it; it is given to us freely. Mercy is all this love of God. This merciful love of God encounters everyone in his poverty and in his need.

In the Latin language the word *mercy* is made up of two words: "misery" and "heart." This is the heart of God that comes to meet every human misery. The wounds of sin, the evil that lives within us from our sadness and our discouragement—all of these are visited by God's mercy. This free and abundant source comes to every man and woman and takes a particular form according to each one's need. Suffering and distress is really the object of God's tenderness. God is the Good Samaritan who comes to take care of our wounds.

So how can Mary help us to understand and welcome this mystery of mercy? I think her role is very important, even if discrete, as it is every time Mary acts. She never takes the front stage;

she always guides us to her Son. Her role is very important, and it's good to entrust ourselves to her and allow her to guide us.

We can talk about many reasons for this, and perhaps the first one is that Mary is the person who is the closest to God. She has the deepest knowledge of God, and it is a knowledge she communicates to us.

St. John Paul II preached at Fatima for the canonization of the children of Fatima. In this homily he recounted one of Mary's apparitions, in which something like a ray of light enveloped the children and plunged them into the mystery of God. He explained that it was divine plan for "a woman clothed with the sun" to come down to earth and visit these small children. St. John Paul II told how her words, so protective and compassionate, were words of "a mother's voice and heart," as she asked these children to offer their lives as "victims of reparation." These children saw light shining from her hands, a light which pierced their souls and allowed them to feel united with God, absorbed in his Love. They felt that His love was a burning fire, burning but not consuming. The Pope likens this experience to that of Moses and the burning bush. God presents His love and protection as a fire, burning out of love for us, and as we welcome his burning love, we become "the dwelling-place and, consequently, a 'burning bush' of the Most High."[1]

I find something very beautiful in these thoughts of the Holy Father. Thanks to Mary these little shepherds without any sort of culture were plunged into the mystery of God. They entered into an awareness of God that can't be expressed with words. They experienced a burning fire that did not consume, just like Moses experienced with the burning bush (see Exodus 3:2) This was a very important moment in the history of Israel because it was really a moment of mercy. "I've seen the misery of my people. I've seen their suffering and this is why I come" (see

---

1. Homily of His Holiness Pope John Paul II at the Beatification of Francisco and Jacinta Marto, Fatima, May 13th, 2000.

Exodus 3:7–8). And God called Moses to save his people.

These poor little shepherds from Portugal lived in grace through Mary. They had an experience of God that was just as profound as Moses experienced, who is one of the greatest characters of the Old Testament. This experience of grace is something that before was reserved for a tiny elite but is now available to everyone.

"I thank thee Father, Lord of heaven and earth, that thou hast hidden these things from the wise and understanding and revealed them to babes" (Matthew 11:25). We recognize that we are very small, but through Mary we can know God in his love and in his infinite mercy.

The very beautiful thirty-first chapter of Jeremiah announces the new covenant and the awareness of God—where everybody will know God, from the smallest to the greatest.

> "This is the covenant which I will make with the house of Israel after those days," says the Lord. "I will put my law within them, and I

will write it upon their hearts, and I will be their God, and they shall be my people. And no longer shall each man teach his neighbor and teach his brother saying, 'Know the Lord.' For they shall all know me from the least of them to the greatest," says the Lord. (Jeremiah 31:33–34)

So nobody will need to teach anybody else? Will all the preachers be out of work because everybody will know God?

"For I will forgive their iniquity, and I will remember their sin no more." (Jeremiah 31:34)

God in his mercy will forgive our sins and won't remember any of our faults. The greatest knowledge of God is the knowledge of his mercy. There is another passage predicting that, during that time, nobody will commit any evil because of the knowledge of God: "For the earth will be filled with the knowledge of the glory of the Lord, as the waters cover the sea" (Habakkuk 2:14). The whole earth will be full of the knowledge of God. This is what our world needs: a time when we know God with our heart, when we know him as a merciful God. We are forgiven and purified, and we, too, become merciful and able to forgive and to love.

## MARY'S ROLE

Mary plays a very important role in this process. She introduces us to the knowledge of God and his mercy, which is his deepest attribute. Mary also has this grace for another reason: she herself knew the mercy of God. Of course she did not sin, and she didn't need forgiveness, but in the Magnificat she sang of the mercy of God.

She knows that this mercy is a gift from God and that it's completely free. God's mercy is a grace given to Mary in advance, by merit of the sacrifice of the cross. The effusion of mercy that springs forth from the cross, from the very heart of Christ, is what purified Mary. Sometimes God shows his mercy in pardoning sins that have been committed, but sometimes he reveals it in advance by pardoning all the sins that we might commit.

We see that aspect of his mercy in St. Thérèse of Lisieux. She was slightly jealous of Mary Magdalene because Mary Magdalene was forgiven much and she really loved Jesus—and Thérèse didn't sin as much as Mary Magdalene, and she wanted to love Jesus more than anybody. She wrote, "Jesus *has forgiven me more than St. Mary Magdalene* since He forgave me *in advance* by preventing me from falling."[2]

> "Therefore I tell you, her sins, which are many, are forgiven, for she has loved much; but he who is forgiven little, loves little." (Luke 7:47)

The more we are holy, the more we depend totally on the mercy of God, either for the sins

---

2. St. Thérèse of Lisieux, *Story of a Soul: The Autobiography of St. Thérèse of Lisieux*, Study Edition (Washington, DC: ICS Publications, 2005).

that are forgiven us or for the good that we do, the more all of this comes from grace. Everything is given and everything comes from the mercy of God, not from our merit but from the free love of God.

Therefore Mary is the richest of all creatures, the holiest and the most beautiful, but also the humblest and the poorest because she knows that she has received everything from God. She has received everything from God freely, and so she gives everything freely. There is nothing left for her—there is only God who passes through her in complete humility and poverty of heart. More than the greatest sinners, Mary knows the mercy of God, and she can help us to understand it in all its depth.

## ACCEPTING AND TRUSTING GOD'S MERCY

We see in the Gospel that the mercy of God is the greatest mystery and the most beautiful treasure. However, we have a difficult time accepting it.

It's not easy to welcome the mercy of God. We see it in the Gospel, and we see it in our daily lives. We have a hard time receiving the mercy of God because we really have very little trust in God's forgiveness.

I'll share a small example. As a priest, I often meet people who say, "A few years ago, I committed this great fault, and I went to confession. I think God forgave me, but I don't seem to be able to forgive myself." I hear this frequently.

This attitude can come about for certain reasons. Perhaps it has to do with human psychology, but without a doubt, there is a lack of trust. We don't really believe in this reality of the forgiveness of God, and so we don't always fully welcome it. God forgives us, but we can't forgive ourselves.

So there is an issue of trust that is not easy for us because of our wounded human nature. Yet we have the witness of the saints who were great prophets of mercy, such as St. Thérèse and St. Faustina, and they all emphasize the importance of trust. What permits us to access God's mercy? Trust—complete trust in God. The greater the trust, the more mercy will be given to us, and the more we will please God.

Thérèse of the Child Jesus said that what wounds the heart of God most are not our faults but our lack of trust in his love. This is what prevents us from receiving the abundant mercy and love of God.

Consider asking yourself the question, "What will allow me to access the mercy of God?" My answer is that there are four conditions. The first one I've already talked about: trust. The more you trust, the more your trust is complete and the more you'll receive this freely-given mercy.

## HUMILITY AND POVERTY OF SPIRIT

The second condition is humility. Sometimes we have a hard time accepting the mercy of God; we don't forgive ourselves even when God forgives us. Sometimes the reason is pride—I don't accept being a person who has fallen, who has made mistakes. I would have liked to have been the perfect person, infallible. But I've made mistakes, and I can't accept having faults. This stems from a certain form of pride.

We have difficulty accepting that we have to depend on the mercy of God. We would like to save ourselves. We would like to be our own richness—to be rich based on our good actions and qualities. We have a hard time accepting that we are poor of heart. To receive everything from the mercy of God—to accept that God is our source of richness and not ourselves—requires a great poverty of heart.

We should cite again a phrase from St. Thérèse of the Child Jesus. She says the following in one of her letters to a priest:

> Ah! how little known is the goodness, the merciful love of Jesus, Brother! . . . It is true, to enjoy these treasures one must humble oneself, recognize one's nothingness, and that is what many souls do not want to do.[3]

---

3. Letter 261 to Fr. Bellière, July 26, 1897.

We see this in the Gospel as well. We sometimes have a hard time accepting the mercy of
God for ourselves, and also accepting it for others. Why was Jesus put to death? Because of the
jealousy of the scribes and Pharisees, who refused
to accept that he could be so merciful and wel-
coming to publicans and sinners.

## JUSTICE VERSUS MERCY

This is the attitude of the older brother in the
Parable of the Prodigal Son (see Luke 15:11–
32). At the end of the younger brother's journey, during which he did many foolish things,
he comes back repentant to his home. His
father is happy to welcome him back. "For this
my son was dead, and is alive again; he was lost,
and is found" (Luke 15:24). The father orders
a feast. The servants kill a fattened calf. The
older brother is furious, and he says, more or
less, "I was always with you, I never did anything wrong, and you never gave me even a kid
goat." He doesn't accept the mercy of the father

toward his younger brother. Why? Because he has his own sense of justice.

This is the problem with the Pharisees. They satisfy their own sense of justice, and they are happy with their own works. They think they have a right to the blessing of God, and when this blessing falls on a sinner, they see it as an injustice and feel that their rights have been taken away.

This is the pretense of human pride, of insisting on our own rights. We can't accept that God would be so generous toward the poor and sinners. But it is better for us to accept this because there's always a moment in our lives where *we* are poor and sinners, when even the greatest people become poor and fall into sin.

We can see an example of this alteration of conditions in the story of the Prophet Elijah. He is powerful: He causes a drought for three years (see 1 Kings 17:1), and in a contest with the pagan priests of Baal, he commands that God rain down fire from heaven to consume the sacrifice on Mount Carmel (see 1 Kings 18:38). Soon after this spectacular triumph, he faces his weakness and poverty. He flees to the desert to escape the wrath of Jezebel. He's discouraged. He seeks shelter from the burning sun, then gives up. He finally says, "It is enough; now O Lord, take away my life; for I am no better than my fathers" (1 Kings 19:4). He is aware of his poverty.

Instead God sends an angel to comfort and feed him, and this enables him to walk for forty days and forty nights and meet God in a new way. This great prophet had his moment of depression. He felt himself to be poor, yet everything he had accomplished was a grace.

Sometimes it's good that we rejoice when we have accomplished great things. But in the moments where we feel our poverty, we should also rejoice, because the good news is for the poor. Mercy is for those who need it, who feel profoundly that they cannot save themselves. Our only hope is not through our own works; it's hope in the infinite mercy of God. That is

our only security. It's our only security in life
to know that the mercy of God will never run
out. That's the second condition for welcom-
ing the mercy of God: humility and poverty
of heart.

## BEING THANKFUL

There is a third important condition: gratitude.
Jesus said in the Gospel, "For to him who has,
will more be given, and he will have abundance;
but from him who has not, even what he has will
be taken away" (Matthew 13:11). We can understand it this way: He who knows he has received
gifts from God, who gives thanks for these gifts,
will receive more.

There is a little secret in the spiritual life: The
more the heart gives thanks, the more God gives,
even when life isn't perfect, even when we don't
have everything we need or want. The more we
thank God, the more our heart is open to receive
even more of his mercy and his gifts.

## FORGIVENESS

The fourth condition to receive God's mercy abundantly is very clear in the Gospel: If you do not forgive, God cannot forgive you. Sometimes what stops us from receiving the mercy of God is our lack of mercy toward others, our hardness of heart toward others, our lack of goodness toward others. And so we too need to be merciful. "Blessed are the merciful, for mercy will be shown them" (Matthew 5:7). The more I'm merciful with my brothers and sisters, the more God will be merciful with me.

Mary can help us with all these four conditions. Do you know the greatest secret that St. Louis de Montfort discovered, and why he came up with the consecration to Mary? Very simply, if you give yourself completely to Mary, she will give herself completely to you. Everything Mary receives—all her graces, her interior disposition toward God—will come to you.

St. Thérèse of the Child Jesus understood this well. She wrote a poem about Mary, "Why

I Love you, O Mary." In it is this sentence: "The treasure of the mother belongs to the child."[4]

There are mothers among you, and I think you know very well that everything a mother possesses is not for her; it's for her children. And Mary is our mother. Everything she receives from God, she gives to us. The more I give myself to Mary, the more she will give herself to me.

## GIFTS OF MARY

Louis de Montfort writes about everything Mary gives us. She gives us her faith, her trust in God. She dilates our hearts in a filial trust. She takes away every fear from us, along with all our suspicions. She gives us trust and simplicity and a profound faith that enables us to place all of our trust in God. So also gives us her humility.

In the same poem written by Thérèse, another line that says, "Close around you, Mary, I love to stay small." There is a mystery here. The closer

---

4. See Appendix II.

we are to Mary, the more we accept our own smallness. When we are faced with ourselves and our smallness, our faults, our wounds, our imperfections, and our failures, we tend to exaggerate our difficulties. But when we're close to Mary, we so understand the goodness of God that we are able to accept our smallness.

Mary's maternal love helps us to recognize and accept peacefully our limitations and fragility. This is Mary's great gift to us. Close to Mary, we love our littleness. Thérèse says this as well: "The more that you love your smallness and your poverty, the more Jesus will give you grace."

Mary gives us the gift of thanksgiving. Mary is the Virgin of the Magnificat. She sings the marvels and the mercy of God in a song of hope. The Magnificat is a song of hope because it's not yet fulfilled. God will strike down the mighty from their thrones and will raise the humble. When Mary sings this, it is not yet fulfilled: the kings are still sitting on their thrones. Mary's song of hope is a song of gratitude. Mary teaches us the grace of thanksgiving and praise through her Magnificat.

If we want to receive mercy, we have to be merciful toward others. Here Mary gives us a beautiful gift: her maternal heart, her merciful heart.

What do we observe about Mary at the wedding at Cana? She's the first one to see the needs of the people around her. There is no more wine; this would be a catastrophe—even worse if this wedding was in France! Mary is the first one to notice, and she goes to find Jesus.

On this opening day of the Year of Mercy, I got a text from someone in Lourdes who went through the Door of Mercy. It's supposed to open next Sunday. But apparently in Lourdes they are ahead of schedule. I think it's the Virgin Mary who arranged that. She's always accelerating things!

What's beautiful about Mary is not only the strength of her faith but the delicacy of her love. How attentive she is, how tender, how much she sees the needs of others, and how much she moves herself to attend to them. She can help us learn to pay attention to others first, recognizing their needs, recognizing their suffering, and recognizing how much they need our pardon or our aid.

Mary can help us open our hearts and eyes to the needs of our brothers and sisters. She motivates us to acts of love and mercy through her maternal grace. Her tenderness and love has the force of faith. It can be compared to an army ready for battle. She's strong against evil, but with an inner peace and tenderness that she transmits to us.

Throughout this Year of Mercy, let us ask for the grace to welcome Mary into our hearts, to give ourselves to her so she can give us what she has received from God. She will give us limitless trust, faith, humility, hope, and thanksgiving, along with her loving and attentive gaze and the goodness that is so deep within her. By practicing all of this with Mary, she will ask for what we need. Mary adds everything we are missing in our faith, and so we receive far beyond our merits.

In entrusting ourselves to Mary, we can live with all abundance the graces of this year. We will better understand the mercy of God, and we will welcome it more for ourselves and for others.

——·∽·——

# Chapter Two

# MERCY AND FORGIVENESS
# IN THE FAMILY

*A homily given on December 9, 2015, at Resurrection*
*Church in Nashua, New Hampshire*

Lord, we wish to thank you for your presence
among us—this presence of mercy, this presence of love and of peace. We thank you for all
the graces you have prepared for us this evening.
We want to entrust ourselves especially to the
Virgin Mary, who brings us into an atmosphere
of prayer and adoration. We ask that she opens
our hearts to the Word of God, in order that she
might bear fruit in us.

Tonight I am going to address the subject of
mercy and forgiveness in the family. How can our

families find grace through this year of mercy? It's a vast subject. I'm going to present a few reflections that I hope will help you.

In addition to each person, families are also called to receive the mercy of God as well as give it. This is the great invitation Pope Francis gives us—to welcome the mercy of God for ourselves and to be merciful to others as the Father is merciful to us.

The family is a very privileged place to live this out. When we live in a family, we live together under the same roof. We have very close relationships; we are physically close. We can both support one another and love one another. We can teach our children. The family is a place of great graces; it is the fundamental unit of the Church.

Because of this closeness of life in families, we also see and experience limitations, both our own and those of others. Take my case, for example. I have lived in a religious community for forty years, and a religious community is a little bit like a family. Before entering, I was convinced that I was very patient, and after fifteen days, I was convinced that my patience wasn't worth very much.

This kind of self-knowledge is one of the graces of family life. We see our limits, our lack of patience, the difficulty we sometimes have in loving and in forgiving. We also see our weaknesses and our faults. In our relationships with others, these weaknesses and faults often come to light. Sometimes there is one child who really pushes me to the limit. Or he makes me so angry so that I see my failures and how much I need mercy and forgiveness for my lack of love. I realize how much I need God's help because alone, I am not able to love. I am not able to count on my own strength. I have to count on the grace of God, on the Holy Spirit who comes to aid my weakness.

When we take family life seriously, when we really want to love those around us, very often we are obliged to ask for this grace from God. We say, "Lord, you see my limits, my hardness of heart, and only you can help me. Only you can heal me and give me the love I need to love others, the love I need to love my wife or my children." Your heart is limited, but thankfully God's is overabundant. He is rich in mercy, and if we ask for this grace, he will help us little by little to truly love. When we live together as a couple or in a family, we see each other's poverty. We're obliged to exercise mercy with each other, to accept and love each other as we are, and to be patient and practice all the works of mercy. Family life gives us a lot of opportunities for this struggle.

We can say a lot of things about this subject, but I would like to speak about two points. The first is forgiveness, which is so important in families, and the second is the way we view others.

Before getting into these points, let's look at a couple passages of Scripture, particularly one of the many invitations of the Gospel to be merciful. St. Matthew uses the sentence, "You, therefore, be perfect, as your heavenly Father is perfect" (Matthew 5:48). Luke formulates it a little differently in Luke 6:36–38:

Be merciful even as your Father is merciful. Judge not, and you will not be judged. Condemn not, and you will not be condemned; forgive, and you will be forgiven; give, and it will be given to you; good measure pressed down, shaken together, running over will be put into your lap. For the measure you give will be the measure you get back.

These are invitations to mercy—to not judging, to not condemning, to forgiving as God forgives us. They also contain a promise of happiness. It's not very easy to live out, but if you live it with God's help, you will be fulfilled, "good measure . . . running over."

Put on then, as God's chosen ones, holy and beloved, compassion, kindness, lowliness, meekness, and patience, forbearing one another and, if one has a complaint against another, forgiving each other; as the Lord has forgiven you, so you also must forgive. And above all these, put on love, which binds everything together in perfect harmony. And let the peace of Christ rule in your hearts to which, indeed, you were called in the one body. And be thankful. (Colossians 3:12–15)

This is an invitation to love that brings peace, a love that is not just an abstraction, but is very concrete—a love of gentleness, goodness, humility, and forgiveness. This passage is really at the heart of the vocation of family life.

## FORGIVENESS IN FAMILY LIFE

I would like to say a few things about forgiveness, because the mercy we practice in family life takes many forms. We encourage, we support, we carry one another. But the most necessary form of mercy is the ability to forgive.

It's not always easy to forgive, but it is necessary. If there is no forgiveness in a couple's relationship, if there is no forgiveness among family members, problems start to multiply. Sufferings of all kinds develop and create walls that separate us from each other. On the other hand, if day after day we forgive, ordinary relations remain possible and love can always be reborn. Forgiveness is not always easy; it is one of the most unselfish acts of love. Forgiveness can also be one of the greatest acts of freedom—the freedom to love even the one who has done you wrong.

When it is hard to forgive, this is a grace we must ask for. Sometimes our human strength is not enough and we must ask God in humility and prayer. Sometimes it takes time to receive this grace, and this is normal. When we're very deeply wounded, receiving this grace can take time and a lot of prayer, patience, and humility. When we have the grace to forgive, all the bad things disappear. Love and communion are reborn.

It is difficult to say, "I forgive you." It is easier to forgive the way Jesus does. When Jesus forgave his enemies on the cross, he turned to the Father and said, "Father, forgive them. They know not what they do" (Luke 23:34).

When we find it too hard to say, "I forgive you," we too must turn to the Father, because in the end only God can really forgive. We have to turn to the Father and say those words of Jesus, "Father, forgive him—or forgive her—because he (or she) doesn't know what he (or she) is doing."

It's true that, most of the time, man doesn't know the evil he is committing. He doesn't really realize the extent of it. To forgive, we have to go through the heart of the Father. This is the source of forgiveness. It is not in me; it's the heart of God, and that's where I have to go looking for forgiveness.

## FORGIVENESS AND FAITH

Forgiveness is an act of love, an act of charity. It is an act of faith as well as an act of hope, because when I forgive somebody, one of the things that allows me to forgive is faith. Otherwise forgiveness would be very hard.

God can convert something good even out of evil. Let's say I've lived through an evil; I have suffered, I was wounded, but I believe that God is powerful enough to bring goodness out of everything, even the evil committed against me.

In the Gospel reading for the Feast of the Immaculate Conception, the angel tells Mary that nothing is impossible for God. If we have faith that God can convert a good thing out of evil—an evil that we've suffered through—then God can heal our wounds, and forgiveness is easier.

In the world today we have a hard time forgiving, and one of the reasons is our lack of faith. We are convinced that our wounds are definitive and will never be healed; we think there is no remedy for evil. This is a very human reaction.

Forgiveness is also an act of hope. When I don't forgive, I'm condemning someone. That means that I'm identifying this person with the evil he or she has committed. I see this person as guilty and bad. I don't want to forgive him or her. I have no hope for this person; I don't think he or she can change.

On the contrary, forgiving someone is a very beautiful act of hope. This person did something bad, he or she committed a wrong act, but I don't want to identify the person with the bad action because God still loves this person who has done something bad. God is working in this person's heart. Perhaps this person will convert. This person I'm judging and condemning will perhaps one day be a great saint. When we look at the lives of the saints, there are assassins, adulterers, criminals, but grace changed their hearts.

## HOPE

When I forgive someone, it is an act of hope. Through forgiving them, I have hope in the path that this person will take. I have hope for this person's progress, this person's conversion. I believe that this person, too, will meet Christ and his or her heart will be transformed.

Hope is very powerful because what we hope for, God will grant. There is a passage from St. Paul that speaks of loving your enemies.

"Don't repay evil with evil, but do good to your enemies" (Romans 12:17). Paul goes on to say: "No, if your enemy is hungry, feed him. If he is thirsty, give him drink. For by so doing, you will heap burning coals upon his head. Do not be overcome by evil, but overcome evil with good" (Romans 12:20–22).

The part about "burning coals" is very strange. When you do something good for your enemy, you heap burning coals on his head? This image of the burning coal goes back to the calling of Isaiah. When Isaiah sees the holiness of God, he feels his great sinfulness. He says, "Woe is me. I have seen the Lord, and I am a man of impurity. I live in the midst of a people of impure lips." A seraph takes a burning coal from the altar with tongs and passes it over Isaiah's lips. He says, "Now your lips are purified and your sin is forgiven" (Isaiah 5:7). This purification with the burning coal is the grace of forgiveness.

When we pile burning coals on someone's head, it means we're preparing an effusion of the

Holy Spirit. One day these coals on the person's head will enter into his heart, not in condemnation but as a purification, as a conversion. If, with hope and faith, I forgive this person, I'm accumulating the Holy Spirit over his or her head. One day, this Holy Spirit will enter in and transform the heart of this person, purifying and sanctifying him or her.

## FORGIVENESS SETS US FREE

I truly believe in the power of hope. Forgiveness is an act of hope because what we hope for, with faith, God will grant. Hope never disappoints.

Furthermore, when we forgive someone, we set that person free of revenge or judgment. But it's not only the other person we set free; it's also ourselves. Every time that I forgive somebody, I set myself free.

What happens when we don't forgive? If someone did something wrong to me ten years ago, and I still don't want to forgive them ten years later, it means I am held prisoner by my past. It is as though a chain is holding me ten years in the past. I am not free to receive the graces of today.

One time I heard something very sad during a parish mission. There was a woman, perhaps ninety years old. We spoke, and the main thing she brought up was that she was still bitter against some religious sisters she said had mistreated her in school when she was ten. It's very sad to see someone who is ninety years old still holding a grudge about something that happened a lifetime ago.

We are not free in regards to the past when we have not forgiven. We can't receive the graces of the present moment, all the blessings God wants to give us. We can't receive them because we are attached to our past by this refusal of forgiveness.

What does it mean not to forgive? It means that I'm holding a grudge, a judgment, sometimes a hatred in my heart. And this poisons my heart. My heart is not pure; it is not free. It's as if I'm carrying poison in myself. This does harm to me for many reasons. Again, it keeps me in a condition of dependence.

These days we talk a lot about emotional dependence. Sometimes we become overly dependent on somebody else. We are not free; we have become too attached to this person. We have made an idol out of that person. We can't live ten minutes without him or her, and we're always texting them on our phones. "Are you thinking about me? Do you love me?"

To hate someone is also a form of dependence. We often think as much about somebody we despise as we do about somebody we love. Our thoughts are occupied with bad experiences, and our heart by negative feelings. I'm dependent on the person I can't forgive.

On the contrary, when I forgive, I am free. I am no longer in this state of dependence. I can be completely myself, and I can allow the grace of God to dwell in me. I can allow positive thoughts and hopes instead of stirring up a poison in myself. Forgiveness sets me free. Be encouraged to ask for the grace of forgiveness and practice it.

Here is another story. A few years ago, a woman on a retreat I was giving came to speak to me. She had a problem. She couldn't forgive her husband. He had deceived her. Her husband had a little adventure with another woman. It hadn't gone on for very long, and it had happened three years before. She felt very wounded, and she couldn't forgive him.

The fact that she was wounded is completely normal. Adultery in a marriage causes real suffering for the innocent spouse. It's infidelity and a betrayal of a couple's communion of will and heart as well as their physical communion and intimacy. To give one's body to someone outside the marriage is to betray the conjugal covenant, so it is very wounding to the one betrayed.

I don't want to justify the husband, but having said this, this woman's feelings had been eating at her for a long time. She was a good Christian. She knew the Gospels; she knew she was called to forgive. She said, "I have read all the books about forgiveness, but I can't do it." We spoke a little bit and I think in the end I understood the real reason—as much as a man can understand a woman!

I saw that there were two reasons blocking her from forgiveness. The first one was this: the fact that her husband had betrayed her was in a certain sense an advantage for her, giving her a comfortable position of superiority on him. She could say as a result, "I'm the saint and he's the sinner, so I'm well above him." She did not want to lose this advantage.

What does it mean to forgive? It demands much humility because it means that there is no saint and sinner. Instead there are two sinners. He sinned against her, which was true, but was she perfect? Had she not sinned against him? Maybe not in such a visible way, but she also had areas in which she was wrong.

What do we do when we forgive? We leave this situation and we come to the same level. Both of us are poor. Both of us are sinners. We forgive one another, and we walk together on the same level. There is no superiority. We are both sinners, and God forgives us both.

We forgive each other as two poor people, without seeking to dominate each other, without believing that we're better than the other. We walk together in humility and in poverty of heart. There is a decision to make, one that requires humility as well as trust in each other, a trust in the marriage.

What is a marriage? It is two poor people, two sinners who welcome one another and walk together without holding each other accountable, without asking who is the worst or who is the best. We don't ask these questions.

I think the woman's second reason for not forgiving was that his sin was very useful. When her husband started to hold his head up high, when he wanted to go out with his friends, she held a grudge against him: "Remember what you did to me." We often use the sin of another, in some way, to keep him or her down as a form of manipulation.

Forgiveness means renouncing the power of reproaching the other person. Forgiveness gives the other person his or her liberty back. It is to this that the Gospel invites us—to cancel our debts.

## Canceling Debts

You do not owe me anything, and I don't ask anything of you, because I have forgiven you and we advance in mutual freedom. I respect your freedom as you respect mine. I don't subtly use the mistakes you have made to oblige you to do this or that.

This canceling of debts is very important in family life because, very often, we want to exert a certain power over each other. "You've done me wrong, so you owe me." Sometimes it's not so much a question of forgiveness, but another type of attitude that behaves in the same way. For example, "I have done many good things for you, I was generous, I helped you out for a long time, so you owe me something. You owe me gratitude. I have a certain power over you because of all the good things I did for you."

Jesus calls us to forgive these debts. If someone does you wrong, forgive. That person doesn't owe you anything. And if you've done something good for someone, you don't demand anything in return. Love freely and not in order to receive something back or to oblige the other person.

This is very important, because if we don't understand this, if we don't forgive *all* these debts, we calculate what we're giving and what we're receiving. We are always keeping tabs, and we are never satisfied. The only way to be satisfied and happy is to love freely, without expecting recompense, to forgive the evil that has been done to us and not demand anything for the good we do to others. This is really the path of freedom of heart.

## AS JESUS LOOKED AT OTHERS

There is a way of looking at people that gives life; it's a gaze of goodness, of mercy, of encouragement and hope. There is also a way of looking at someone that can bring death—a look that accuses, that closes, that judges, that rejects. Pope Francis preached on the gaze of Jesus in a homily that he gave on September 21, the Feast of St. Matthew.

You know the story of the conversion of St. Matthew. He was a publican, a tax collector who worked for the Romans in a way that was doubtlessly dishonest. He was despised. One day he was with a group of his fellow tax collectors when Jesus passed by. Jesus looked at him and called him, this man the whole world had judged as despicable. Jesus looked at him with love, and he chose him to become an apostle.

Pope Francis's homily focuses on the meaning of this gaze of Jesus, this gaze of mercy and hope, that sets us free. He says, as Jesus looked at Matthew the tax collector, with the powerful gaze of love, it moved Matthew to change his life forever. As a tax collector, who took from the Jews to hand over to the Romans, Matthew was shunned, despised, thought of as a traitor who "extorted from [his] own." Pope Francis says that no one prayed, ate, or even spoke to such as these . . . but Jesus did. He stopped and looked at Matthew with peace, with mercy, with calm, with a gaze that Matthew had never experienced. And, Pope Francis tells us, "this look unlocked Matthew's heart; it set him free, it healed him, it gave him hope, a new life," and Jesus looks at us this way too. Jesus looks at us first, he invites us in, he makes no fuss over our sinfulness. As Pope Francis so beautifully says, He sees "beyond appearances, beyond sin, beyond failures and unworthiness." Our wealth, our stature: Jesus doesn't care. What He gazes at intently is our dignity which stands through the test of our fallen nature, our brokenness, and "endures in the depth of our soul."[1]

The Pope says that Jesus sees further than sin. He sees deeper than our wounds. He sees the child of God within us. He sees our dignity as children of God. And in looking at us, he sets this child of God free. He opens up a path of freedom by looking at us with love. No matter what our sin, no matter our poverty, Jesus looks at us with tenderness. In this look, he purifies us, he gives us hope, and he opens us

1. This text is taken from the Vatican translation of the Pope's homily on his apostolic visit to Cuba, September 2015.

up to a path of life. The Pope reminds us that Jesus came to earth so that all of us, who feel unworthy, could experience His gaze of love. This gaze is the source of our hope and our joy, which propels our faith and ignites our love.

Let us allow ourselves to be looked at by Jesus with this look of mercy that does not judge us but instead sees our identity as children of God and encourages and raises us up.

I suggest that you to take a few minutes of silence. I invite you to look at Jesus, who is here in a true way in the Eucharist. Look at him with faith, with hope, and with love.

What is more important, let Jesus look at you. Place yourselves within the gaze of Jesus and welcome this gaze that looks at *you* peacefully and calmly, that loves you and sees your deepest identity. Jesus, who looks at us with hope and who, in so looking at us, loves us, heals us, and purifies us. Jesus encourages us to live our lives as children of God.

Let us take these moments to look at Jesus with faith and, most of all, to welcome his gaze and allow ourselves to be healed by it, to be healed of our discouragements, all the ways in which we feel guilty, our worries, maybe our shame. This gaze of Jesus can heal everything in us; it can purify and renew everything in our hearts.

It's only a question of one thing: to allow ourselves to be looked at the way Jesus looked at Matthew. To allow ourselves to be seen. Every time Jesus looks at us, he sets us free; he gives us a new life. Let us allow Jesus to look at us.

Chapter Three

—⋅✍⋅—

# MERCY AND TRUST IN ST. THÉRÈSE OF LISIEUX

*A homily given on December 10, 2015, at*
*St. Patrick's Church, Pelham, New Hampshire*

I can't say enough about St. Thérèse of Lisieux (1873–1897). She entered the convent at Carmel at age fifteen, and died at twenty-four—she lived a very short but intense life. After her death, her writings—including her autobiography, letters, and poems—spread rapidly throughout the world. Millions of hearts have been touched by her message. A few weeks before her death, she said, *I will spend my Heaven doing good on Earth.*

One of her favorite themes was the mercy of God. And this was at a time marked by Jansenism, which consisted of an exaggerated view of God's severity and justice in a way that made people afraid. On the other hand, Thérèse focused on what is essential in the Gospels: the love of God as expressed by a tender father who loves and heals each of his children.

Thérèse helped millions of people to rediscover the fatherhood of God. She was canonized in 1925, only twenty-eight years after her death. St. John Paul II even proclaimed her a Doctor of the Church in 1997. This is fairly surprising: a young girl who never did any theological studies is now Doctor of the Church. And we are invited to enter her school.

I'm going to speak on mercy according to Thérèse. First, Thérèse experienced the mercy of God in her own life, and then she brought it to others. She started writing her autobiography two years before her death at the request of her superiors. They could sense that she was living through something very beautiful, something important not to lose. Let us also ask the grace of looking at each other in our family life with the same merciful gaze that God has for us. May my look on others give them freedom and hope, as Jesus does for me.

## A WIDER VISION OF MERCY

In the beginning Thérèse wasn't very enthusiastic to obey this request because she was reticent to have others centered on her and her life. But very quickly she understood that doing so was a grace because by writing the story of her life, she was, in fact, going to tell others about the mercy of God.

In the first chapter of her autobiography, *The Story of a Soul*, Thérèse says she will tell the effect of God's mercy on her soul. How does she describe this mercy of God? She says he accompanied her. He helped her to grow. He spoke to her heart with love. He was there throughout her life. Even when she suffered, the living presence of God supported and encouraged her and forgave her sins. She understood the mercy of God not only for herself, but for the whole world—and not just the forgiveness of sins as we tend to think of mercy. To Thérèse it was much more than that.

To understand Thérèse's view of mercy, look again at how she saw Mary Magdalene. Like I had pointed out, Thérèse was somewhat jealous of St. Mary Magdalene, who loved Jesus so much because so much had been forgiven of her. The more we forgive someone, the more they're loved, and Thérèse wanted to love Jesus to a point of madness.

One day Thérèse understood that the Lord had forgiven her more than Mary Magdalene, even if she did not sin in the same way. This is what she said:

> The profound words of our Lord to Simon resound with a great sweetness in my soul. I know that he to whom less is forgiven loves less, but I also know that Jesus has forgiven me more than St. Mary Magdalene, since he forgave me in advance by preventing me from falling.

Not only does God forgive us our sins, but he also can strengthen us from committing them.

I wish I could explain what I feel. Here is an example which will express my thoughts at least a little. Suppose a clever physician's child meets with a stone in his path which causes him to fall and break a limb. His father comes to him immediately, picks him up lovingly, takes care of this hurt, using all the resources of his profession for this. His child, completely cured, shows his gratitude. This child is no doubt right in loving his father! But I am going to make another comparison. The father, knowing there is a stone in his child's way, hastens ahead of him and removes it but without anyone's seeing him do it. Certainly, this child, the object of his father's tender foresight, but UNAWARE of the misfortune from which he was delivered by him, will no thank him and will love him less than if he had been cured by him. But if he should come to learn the danger from which he escaped, will he not love his father more?[1]

Therese experienced this mercy in her own life, but she also saw the mercy that God had toward others, which is where she gains a much wider vision of God's mercy.

When Thérèse was fourteen, a little before she entered Carmel, she was already full of love for God. She felt the need to pray for souls, that the redemption of Jesus on the cross would touch all souls without exception, that no person would be lost. She learned about a murderer in Paris, who had killed three people. Thérèse was touched with pity for this man, because he had not repented. He was very arrogant with the judges, and he didn't want to see a priest. She said, "He can't go to hell. I'll pray for him." She prayed. She sacrificed. She had Masses said. She asked her sister, Céline, to pray with her, and she was certain that Jesus would do something.

---

1. See Appendix II.

But it appeared that nothing was happening. This man, Pranzini, was still obstinate. He was condemned to death. At the last minute, as he ascended the scaffold just before being executed, he took a cross and kissed it.

Thérèse saw this in the newspaper the next day, and it stunned her. God had heard her prayer. This is what she said:

My prayer was answered to the letter! In spite of Papa's prohibition that we read no papers, I didn't think I was disobeying when reading the passages pertaining to Pranzini.

The day after his execution, I found the newspaper, La Croix. I opened it quickly and what did I see? Ah! my tears betrayed my emotion and I was obliged to hide. Pranzini had not gone to confession. He had mounted the scaffold and was preparing to place his head in the formidable opening, when suddenly, seized by an inspiration, he turned, took hold of the crucifix the priest was holding out to him and kissed the sacred wounds

three times! Then his soul went to receive the
merciful sentence of Him who declares that in
heaven there will be more joy over one sinner
who does penance than over ninety-nine just
who have no need of repentance![2]

Thérèse cried with joy and emotion to see the
repentance of this man at the last second. She understood the power of prayer, that she, little Thérèse,
who couldn't do very much other than ask, God
had fulfilled her request and this man was saved.

When the newspapers referred to Pranzini,
they said, "This criminal, this monster . . ." But
when Thérèse talked about him in *The Story of
a Soul*, she called him "my first child," the first
man that she saved through her prayer.

## MERCY AND JUSTICE

Sometimes we tend to oppose mercy and justice.
On the other hand, Thérèse united them. In a

---

2. St. Thérèse of Lisieux, *Story of a Soul: The Autobiography of
St. Thérèse of Lisieux*, Study Edition (Washington, DC: ICS Publications, 2005).

letter she wrote to a priest, a missionary she was praying for, she said:

> I know, too, that the Lord is infinitely just, and it is this justice, which frightens so many souls, that is the object of my joy and confidence.
>
> There are people who are very afraid of the justice of God, and for me, it's not the same. The justice of God actually causes me to trust, and this is why.
>
> To be just is not only to exercise severity in order to punish the guilty. It is also to recognize right intentions and to reward virtue. I expect as much from God's justice as from His mercy. It is because He is just that He is compassionate and filled with gentleness, slow to punish, and abundant in mercy, for He knows our frailty. He remembers we are only dust. As a father has tenderness for his children, so the Lord has compassion on us.

The path to perfection is very simple. It's a question of two things: to recognize my nothingness and to abandon oneself as a child into the arms of the Father.

> I leave to great souls and lofty minds the beautiful books I cannot understand, much less put into practice and I rejoice that I am little because children alone and those who resemble them will be admitted to the heavenly banquet.[3]

What Thérèse understood is important. This trust allows her to receive all of God's mercy. The greater our trust, the more God gives us his love. On the contrary, what is most offensive to God is our *not* trusting him. Even if we're poor and imperfect, thanks to our trust, we can touch the heart of God and obtain from him every necessary thing. God does not resist his children's trust.

Thérèse was praying for another missionary priest, a man who was fearful and scrupulous. She invited him to have greater faith in God,

---

3. Letter 226 to Fr. Roulland, May 9, 1897.

even though he was imperfect and weak. In a letter she wrote to him, Thérèse made up a little
story about two children. What she wanted to
show with this story is how much trust touches
the heart of the Father:

> I picture a father who has two children, mis-
> chievous and disobedient, and when he comes
> to punish them, he sees one of them who
> trembles and gets away from him in terror,
> having, however, in the bottom of his heart,
> the feeling that he deserves to be punished.
>
> His brother, on the contrary, throws him-
> self into his father's arms, saying that he is
> sorry for having caused him trouble, that he
> loves him, and to prove it, he will be good
> from now on. If this child asks his father to
> punish him with a kiss, I do not believe that
> the heart of the happy father could resist this
> child, whose sincerity and love he knows.

The audacity of this child! He throws himself
into the arms of his father, and he says, "I ask you
to forgive me. What I did was wrong, but you

know I love you, and I would like to start over again." This child is so audacious that he says to his father, "Punish me with a kiss." What is the father going to do? He can't resist this. This is what Thérèse said:

> He realizes, however, that more than once his son will fall into the same faults. But he is prepared to pardon him always if his son always takes him by his heart.

This was spoken by a Doctor of the Church. The father will always be ready to forgive if this child takes him by the heart. So we have to take God by the heart. God is infinitely powerful, but he has a weak point, and it's his heart. His father's love wants to save and wants to heal, and he takes pleasure in forgiving. Of course, it requires that we have good will and a real desire to correct ourselves, and a true love for the Father. But even if we often fall, every time the Father forgives us. It's this childlike trust in the love of the Father.

I say nothing to you about the first trial, dear little brother. You must know whether his father can love him as much and treat him with the same indulgence as the other.[4]

## THE TRUE FOUNDATION OF TRUST

The more trust we have in God, the more he will love us and give us his grace. We've just spoken of the importance of trust, but what is its foundation? What do we base it on? Because sometimes we can be deluded. We think we trust God, but it is not really a trust in God. It's more of a trust in ourselves.

Let's look at an exemplary Catholic, who behaves well, who is a good example, who trusts God. Then this same person suddenly falls into some sin that really humbles him. He is discouraged and sad. His trust in God is diminished. Now there is not much trust left because he feels that he is a poor sinner after all.

---

4. Letter 258 to Fr. Bellière, July 18, 1897.

What does his reaction mean? It means that "trust in God" was not a trust in God, but a trust in himself, in his works. When you are happy with your own works, you have trust in God. When you have stumbled to the ground, your confidence disappears. That is not trust in God, because God does not change.

What is true trust in God? It is trust that relies on God alone, on his mercy, and not on one's own works. This means that when I'm fragile and poor, when I fall, I don't become discouraged, and I maintain the same trust.

This is not always easy because we are very centered on ourselves instead of only being centered on God. We spend a lot of time measuring ourselves. "Have I made much spiritual progress? Am I in the third or the sixth dwelling of St. Teresa of Avila?"[5] I'm not saying this is a bad question, but what isn't good is to be constantly examining ourselves with the worry and fear of not being at the top.

---

5. Referring to the six stages of spiritual growth described in St. Teresa of Avila's book, *Interior Castle*.

Of course, we need encouragement to practice virtue, so we do have to make an examination of conscience, but what is important is reminding ourselves that true trust relies on God alone and not on our own works.

At the end of *The Story of a Soul*, there is something surprising. Thérèse was very sick with the tuberculosis that was about to kill her. Very tired, she found it hard time to write, and the last lines were written in pencil. What Thérèse talked about in her last words is the foundation of trust.

> Most of all, I imitate the conduct of Magdalene. Her loving audacity, which charms the heart of Jesus, also attracts my own. Yes, I feel it. Even though I had on my conscience all the sins that can be committed, I would go, my heart broken with sorrow, and throw myself into Jesus' arms, for I know how much He loves the prodigal child who returns to Him. It is not because God in His anticipating mercy has preserved my soul from mortal sin that I go to Him with confidence and love.

It's not because God has protected her soul from mortal sin that she went to God in trust and love. She said a little while before this, "Even if I committed every crime that is possible to commit, I would have the same trust, and I would still go and throw myself into the arms of God, asking of course for forgiveness, but certain of being forgiven."

Even after she stopped writing, Thérèse said a couple words. She said them verbally, and they were reported to us:

> Even if I had committed every possible crime, I would have the same confidence. My trust is not in my works. It is in the mercy of God. Even if I felt that I was the worst sinner, I would still throw myself into the arms of God with trust and love, and I know He will forgive me. I know that all of my sins will be as a drop of water in an immense fire, that the love of God is so powerful that it can burn all of my faults if I throw myself into His love.

This trust in God is really the foundation of spiritual life. It's not the acts of man, but the grace of God. Of course, we have to respond to his grace. Thérèse wanted to be a saint. She was generous, she practiced virtue, but where did she place her trust? In God, not in her own works. Thérèse also understood that, to receive all the mercy of God, trust is necessary.

But it also requires humility, to recognize our smallness. We can't both count on the mercy of God and on ourselves and our own works. It's one or the other. Counting on ourselves and glorifying ourselves in our works was the sin of the Pharisees. Thérèse put herself on the side of the publicans, who knew they were poor but who prayed to God and put all their hope in the mercy of God.

What sometimes blocks us from receiving mercy from God is our lack of trust, but it is also our lack of humility. We are not poor of heart. We want to save ourselves rather than welcome everything as a gift from God.

This is what Thérèse says in one of her letters:

Oh, how little known are the goodness, the merciful love of Jesus. Brother, it is true, to enjoy these treasures, one must humble oneself, recognize one's nothingness, and that is what many souls do not want to do.[6]

So to receive all the mercy of God, we have to be humble, make ourselves small, recognize that everything comes from God, and accept dependence on the mercy of God. All our riches are not our own or what we create. Our riches are the love of God for us. This does not mean that we sit around. We have to do all that we can. But our trust, our security, and our hope is the mercy of God.

A few weeks before her death, Thérèse experienced a moment of impatience with her sister. She went to ask her forgiveness. Here is what she said afterward:

Oh, how happy I am to see myself imperfect and to have such need of God's mercy at the moment of my death.

---

6. Letter 261 to Fr. Bellière, July 26, 1897.

And a few days later, this is what she said:

> We experience such great peace when we're totally poor, when we depend on nothing except God.[7]

## POVERTY OF HEART

The more we rely on God alone, which is true poverty of heart, the more we'll find peace. The fact of finding oneself completely poor and totally dependent on the love of God gives us a great peace because God cannot leave us alone. Alone we might struggle, but God can never abandon us. Always have trust in God, but with humility and poverty of heart.

Let's look at someone else: St. Benedict (480–547). In *The Rule of Saint Benedict*, there is a chapter called "The Instruments of Good Works." It's a like a monk's toolbox— everything that a good monk needs. There are

---

7. *St. Thérèse of Lisieux*, Her Last Conversations (Washington, DC: ICS Publications, 1977).

seventy-seven points. It starts with the basic things: love God and one another, don't kill, don't steal. Afterward there are rules that are a little more refined.

The very last point is never to despair of the mercy of God. In the monk's toolbox it may be the most useful tool. When all the other tools haven't worked, there is still this last tool for my salvation: Never despair of the mercy of God.

There is much wisdom in this. But what does it mean? It means do good things and encourage yourself to progress. Try to be a good person with everything that means in practice. If it works, give thanks to God. But when you're faced with your poverty, with your failures and your sin, don't despair. Place your trust in the mercy of God, and he will come to your aid. Although there are many centuries of distance between St. Benedict and Thérèse, it's the same message, and I think it's also important for us.

## RECEIVE AND GIVE MERCY

There is another interesting point about the life of St. Thérèse: She wasn't content just to receive mercy; she also practiced it. The more her love grew, the more merciful she became.

Even while she prayed a great deal for priests, for sinners, for the Church, and for missionaries, she practiced charity toward the other sisters in her community. In her Carmel convent lived a sister with a very irritating personality. None of the sisters wanted to work with her, except Thérèse. She wanted to be merciful and to be close to this sister.

She said that the most wounded souls are the most difficult to live with, but they are also the ones who need the most love. She said that charity is like a lamp, and Jesus tells us we can't hide the lamp. Our charity has to light the way for everybody in the house, so nobody is excluded from our charity and our love. Pope Francis reminds us that the mercy of God is an immense grace that is given to us. But it is also a call; it is also a demand: to be merciful with each other.

Two years before her death, Thérèse came to understand more and more of this mercy of God and how much she wanted to communicate this understanding to others. She felt called to give herself to this mercy and to offer herself totally to make it known—to burn, as it were, with this mercy, like a sacrifice burning on an altar.

Thérèse explained how she received this call. During the time that Thérèse lived, there were some people who offered themselves to God as victims but with the following idea: "I'm going to accept and take on all the chastisements of divine justice for sinners." Thérèse said, "Well, that's very good to do that. It's very generous. But this is not what I feel called to live. I really want to glorify the mercy of God, which is not known enough." This is what she said:

> I was thinking about the souls who offer themselves as victims of God's justice in order to turn away the punishments reserved

to sinners, drawing them upon themselves. This offering seemed great and very generous to me, but I was far from feeling attracted to making it. From the depths of my heart, I cried out, "Oh, my God, will Your justice alone find souls willing to immolate themselves as victims? Does not Your merciful love need them, too?

This is the great suffering of Thérèse: that the love of God is so little known and so little accepted. So many people are closed up, or are fleeing in fear, instead of being totally open to his love and giving themselves totally to him. She continues:

It seems to me that if You were to find souls offering themselves as victims of Holocaust to Your love, you would consume them rapidly. It seems to me, too, that You would be happy not to hold back the waves of infinite tenderness within You. If Your justice loves to release itself, this justice which extends only over the earth, how much more does Your merciful love desire to set souls of fire, since Your mercy reaches to the Heavens?[8]

There are floods of love in God—oceans of tenderness wanting to spill forth over the world but unfortunately not welcomed. So Thérèse gave herself to God so that the world might welcome the love and mercy of God.

This could be also our prayer: "Lord, may the fire of your love and mercy burn in my heart, that it might purify and renew me so I can communicate it to the world." Remember the words of Jesus, "I have come to bring fire to the world" (Luke 12:49).

An immensity of love lives in the heart of God, infinitely larger than anything we could imagine. How much God wants to spread this love! He needs us to welcome this mercy. It is not a question of doing extraordinary penitence;

---

8. St. Thérèse of Lisieux, *Story of a Soul: The Autobiography of St. Thérèse of Lisieux*, Study Edition (Washington, DC: ICS Publications, 2005).

it doesn't mean suffering any more than we have to, but it does require loving more and receiving more of his love with a greater trust, in order to give this love in greater freedom and a greater generosity of heart.

This is the action of God. It is a question of saying yes, of desiring it, of putting our hearts into the hands of God and asking for this fire of love and mercy.

We don't always feel it. But it is not a question of how we feel; it's a question of faith. We should pray: "I believe in your love. I want to live by your love so that the world can be healed, because only your love and your mercy can heal the wounds of man today."

God wants to heal all violence and evil. We offer God our hearts so he can pass through us to visit the whole world.

Appendix I

———·✑·———

# QUOTATIONS ON DIVINE MERCY FROM ST. FAUSTINA (1905–1938)

*St. Faustina is a Polish saint who joined the Congregation of the Sisters of Our Lady of Mercy after the First World War. She received the vision and message of the Lord's Divine Mercy and she was commanded to spread it worldwide. After her death, her diary, Divine Mercy in My Soul, became the source and reference of the Church's devotion to the Divine Mercy.*[1]

## 1. My Heart is a Sea of Mercy

Today the Lord said to me, "I have opened My Heart as a living fountain of mercy. Let all souls draw life from it. Let them approach this sea of

_____

1. St. Faustina Kowalska, *Diary: Divine Mercy in my Soul* (Stockbridge, Mass.: Marians of the Immaculate Conception: 1999).

mercy with great trust. Sinners will attain justi-
fication, and the just will be confirmed in good.
Whoever places his trust in My mercy will be
filled with My divine peace at the hour of death."

The Lord said to me, "My daughter, do not
tire of proclaiming My mercy. In this way you
will refresh this Heart of Mine, which burns with
a flame of pity for sinners. Tell My priests that
hardened sinners will repent on hearing their
words when they speak about My unfathomable
mercy, about the compassion I have for them in
My Heart. To priests who proclaim and extol My
mercy, I will give wondrous power; I will anoint
their words and touch the hearts of those to
whom they will speak."

## 2. No One Have I Excluded

Today the Lord said to me, "My daughter, My
pleasure and delight, nothing will stop Me from
granting you graces. Your misery does not hinder
My mercy. My daughter, write that the greater
the misery of a soul, the greater its right to My
mercy; urge all souls to trust in the unfathomable

abyss of My mercy, because I want to save them all. On the cross, the fountain of My mercy was opened by the lance for all souls—no one have I excluded!"

### 3. Conversations of the Merciful God with a Sinful Soul

**Soul:** Lord, I recognize your holiness, and I fear You.

**Jesus:** My child, do you fear the God of Mercy? My holiness does not prevent Me from being merciful. Behold, for you I have established a throne of mercy on earth—the tabernacle—and from this throne I desire to enter into your heart. I am not surrounded by a retinue or guards. You can come to me at any moment, at any time; I want to speak to you and desire to grant you grace.

**Soul:** Lord, I doubt that You will pardon my numerous sins; my misery fills me with friend.

**Jesus:** My mercy is greater than your sins and those of the entire world. Who can measure the extrent of my goodness? For you I descended from heaven to earth; for you I allowed myself to be nailed to the cross; for you I let me Sacred Heart be pierced with a lance, thus opening wide the source of mercy for you. Come, then, with trust to draw graces from this fountain. I never reject a contrite heart. Your misery has disappeared in the depths of My mercy. Do not argue with Me about your wretchedness. You will give me pleaseure if you hand over to me all your troubles and griefs. I shall heap upon you the treasures of My grace.

## 4. Make an Appeal to my Mercy

Let the greatest sinners place their trust in My mercy. They have the right before others to trust in the abyss of My mercy. My daughter, write about My mercy towards tormented souls. Souls that make an appeal to My mercy delight Me. To such souls I grant even more graces than they ask. I cannot punish even the gretest sinner if he makes an appeal to My compassion, but on the contrary, I justify him in My unfathomable and inscrutable mercy. Write: before I come as a just Judge, I first open wide the door of My mercy. He who refuses to pass through the door of My mercy must pass through the door of My justice . . .

## 5. Prayer to Be Merciful to Others

O Most Holy Trinity! As many times as I breathe, as many times as my heart beats, as many times as my blood pulsates through my body, so many thousand times do I want to glorify Your mercy.

I want to be completely transformed into Your mercy and to be Your living reflection, O Lord. May the greatest of all divine attributes, that of Your unfathomable mercy, pass through my heart and soul to my neighbor.

Help me, O Lord, that my eyes may be merciful, so that I may never suspect or judge from appearances, but look for what is beautiful in my neighbors' souls and come to their rescue.

Help me, that my ears may be merciful, so that I may give heed to my neighbors' needs and not be indifferent to their pains and moanings.

Help me, O Lord, that my tongue may be merciful, so that I should never speak negatively of my neighbor, but have a word of comfort and forgiveness for all.

Help me, O Lord, that my hands may be merciful and filled with good deeds, so that I may do only good to my neighbors and take upon myself the more difficult and toilsome tasks.

Help me, that my feet may be merciful, so that I may hurry to assist my neighbor, overcoming my own fatigue and weariness. My true rest is in the service of my neighbor.

Help me, O Lord, that my heart may be merciful so that I myself may feel all the sufferings of my neighbor. I will refuse my heart to no one. I will be sincere even with those who, I know, will abuse my kindness. And I will lock myself up in the most merciful Heart of Jesus. I will bear my own suffering in silence. May Your mercy, O Lord, rest upon me.

You Yourself command me to exercise the three degrees of mercy. The first: the act of mercy, of whatever kind. The second: the word of mercy—if I cannot carry out a work of mercy, I will assist by my words. The third: prayer—if I cannot show mercy by deeds or words, I can always do so by prayer. My prayer reaches out even there where I cannot reach out physically.

O my Jesus, transform me into Yourself, for You can do all things.

## Appendix II

―⦁∽⦁―

# QUOTATIONS FROM ST. THÉRÈSE DE LISIEUX (1873–1897)

*St. Thérèse de Lisieux, also known as the "Little Flower," was a cloistered Carmelite in Lisieux, France. She is known for her journal, published posthumously, Story of a Soul, as well as a collection of letters, which revealed her incredible yet simple love of Jesus. Her "Little Way" to holiness is a spiritual structure of childlike simplicity that has influenced countless faithful in their journey to know and love Christ. St. Thérèse was made Doctor of the Church by Pope John Paul II.*

## 1. Excerpt of Poem #50, "Pourquoi Je T'aime, Ô Marie" ("Why I love you, O Mary")[1]

Oh! I love you, Mary, saying you are the servant
Of the God whom you charm by your humility.
This hidden virtue makes you all-powerful.
It attracts the Holy Trinity into your heart.
Then the Spirit of Love covering you with his
    shadow,
The Son equal to the Father became incarnate
    in you,
There will be a great many of his sinner brothers,
Since he will be called: Jesus, your
    first-born! . . .

O beloved Mother, despite my littleness,
Like you I possess The All-Powerful within me.
But I don't tremble in seeing my weakness;
The treasures of a mother belong to her child,
And I am your child, O my dearest Mother.
Aren't your virtues and your love mine too?
So when the white Host comes into my heart,

---

1. Kinney, Donald (trans.), *The Poetry of Saint Thérèse of Lisieux* (Washington, DC: ICS Publications, 1996).

Jesus, your Sweet Lamb, thinks he is resting
    in you! . . .

You make me feel that it's not impossible
To follow in your footsteps, O Queen of the
    elect.
You made visible the narrow road to Heaven
While always practicing the humblest virtues.
Near you, Mary, I like to stay little.
I see the vanity of greatness here below.
At the home of Saint Elizabeth, receiving your
    visit,
I learn how to practice ardent charity.

There, Sweet Queen of angels, I listen, delighted,
To the sacred canticle springing forth from your
    heart.
You teach me to sing divine praises,
To glory in Jesus my Savior.
Your words of love are mystical roses
Destined to perfume the centuries to come.
In you the Almighty has done great things.
I want to ponder them to bless him for them.

## 2. *Story of a Soul: The Autobiography of St. Thérèse de Lisieux*[2]

I know that without Him, I could have fallen as low as St. Mary Magdalene, and the profound words of Our Lord to Simon resound with a great sweetness in my soul. I know that *"he to whom less is forgiven, LOVES less,"* but I also know that Jesus *has forgiven me more than St. Mary Magdalene* since He forgave me *in advance* by preventing me from falling. Ah! I wish I could explain what I feel. Here is an example which will express my thoughts at least a little. Suppose a clever physician's child meets with a stone in his path which causes him to fall and break a limb. His father comes to him immediately, picks him up lovingly, takes care of this hurt, using all the resources of his profession for this. His child, completely cured, shows his gratitude. This child is no doubt right in loving his

---

2. St. Thérèse of Lisieux, *Story of a Soul: The Autobiography of St. Thérèse of Lisieux*, Study Edition (Washington, DC: ICS Publications, 2005).

father! But I am going to make another compar-ison. The father, knowing there is a stone in his child's way, hastens ahead of him and removes it but without anyone's seeing him do it. Certainly, this child, the object of his father's tender fore-sight, but UNAWARE of the misfortune from which he was delivered by him, will not thank him and *will love him less* than if he had been cured by him. But if he should come to learn the danger from which he escaped, *will he not love his father more?* Well, I am this child, the object of the *foreseeing love of a Father* who has not sent His Word to save the *just*, but *sinners*. He wants me to *love* Him because he *has forgiven* me not much but ALL. He has not expected me to *love Him much* like Mary Magdalene, but He has willed that I KNOW how He has loved me with a love of *unspeakable foresight* in order that now I may love Him unto *folly!* I have heard it said that one cannot meet a pure soul who loves more than a repentant soul; ah! how I would wish to give the lie to this statement!